I0697747

Contents

Chapter 1: Introduction to Digital Advertising

In the dynamic landscape of marketing and advertising, a fundamental shift has occurred with the rise of the digital era. Chapter 1 sets the stage for our journey into digital advertising, providing a foundational understanding of its significance.

Understanding the Evolution of Advertising

Before delving into the intricacies of digital advertising, it's essential to comprehend how advertising has evolved over time. We'll trace the historical roots of advertising, from ancient signage to the golden age of television commercials. By understanding the evolution of advertising, you'll gain a deeper appreciation of the profound changes that have shaped the industry.

By understanding how advertising has evolved over time, you'll gain a deeper appreciation for the digital advertising landscape we have today. We'll explore the significant milestones, key players, and impactful campaigns that have shaped the world of advertising.

Step-by-Step Evolution:

Step 1: The Birth of Advertising in Ancient Times

Advertising has roots dating back to ancient civilizations. Cave paintings, town criers, and town criers are some of the earliest forms of advertising. For example, ancient Egyptians used papyrus to create posters promoting goods and services.

Step 2: The Gutenberg Press and the Print Revolution

The invention of the printing press by Johannes Gutenberg in the 15th century marked a significant leap in advertising. It allowed for the mass production of printed materials, such as broadsides and posters, spreading information and advertisements more widely.

Step 3: The Rise of Mass Media and Early Brands

The 19th and early 20th centuries witnessed the growth of mass media, including newspapers, magazines, and radio. Iconic brands like Coca-Cola emerged during this period and used advertising to establish brand recognition.

Step 4: The Golden Age of Television Advertising

The mid-20th century brought television into homes, leading to the Golden Age of advertising. Memorable campaigns like the "I Love Lucy" and "Mad Men" series demonstrated the power of TV advertising in reaching vast audiences.

Step 5: The Digital Revolution and the Internet Age

The late 20th century introduced the Internet, revolutionizing advertising once again. Banner ads, email marketing, and the first online search engines (like Yahoo!) emerged. Companies like Amazon and eBay thrived by leveraging the online space for e-commerce.

Step 6: Social Media and the Mobile Advertising Boom

Social media platforms like Facebook, Twitter, and Instagram have become advertising giants, offering precise targeting and engagement with billions of users. The proliferation of mobile devices has created a massive market for mobile advertising.

Step 7: Programmatic Advertising and Data-Driven Marketing

Advances in technology have enabled programmatic advertising, allowing for real-time, data-driven, and automated ad buying. Advertisers can now target specific demographics and even individual users based on their online behavior.

Step 8: The Future: AI, AR, and Interactive Advertising

We look to the future, where artificial intelligence (AI), augmented reality (AR), and interactive advertising are shaping the landscape. Personalized, immersive, and data-driven experiences are at the forefront of advertising innovation.

Each step in this evolution is marked by significant changes in technology, media, and consumer behaviour. Understanding this evolution is crucial for navigating the complex world of digital advertising and crafting effective campaigns that resonate with modern audiences.

The Digital Revolution: Why It Matters

The digital revolution has transformed the way businesses connect with their audience. This section explores the factors that led to this transformation, including the internet's explosive growth, the proliferation of smartphones, and the power of social media. We'll discuss why this shift is so significant, not only for businesses but also for consumers.

In this section, we explore the profound transformation that the digital revolution has brought to the way businesses connect with their audience, and why this shift is not only significant for businesses but also for consumers.

The digital revolution has altered the very fabric of our society, redefining the way we communicate, access information, and make purchasing decisions. In this section, we delve into the reasons why this revolution is a game-changer for businesses and consumers alike.

Unprecedented Reach: The digital era has granted businesses the ability to reach a global audience like never before. With the power of the internet, businesses can connect with potential customers around the world, breaking down geographical barriers. For instance, consider the rise of e-commerce giants like Amazon, which deliver products to doorsteps worldwide, fundamentally changing how we shop.

Personalization: Digital platforms allow businesses to collect and analyze vast amounts of data, enabling highly personalized marketing. This means that consumers now receive tailored recommendations and content based on their preferences and behavior. Companies like Netflix and Spotify are excellent examples of how personalization has enhanced the consumer experience, making content and music suggestions more relevant to individual tastes.

Real-Time Interaction: The digital revolution has introduced the concept of real-time communication. Businesses can engage with customers instantaneously through social media, chat, and email. This shift enables companies to address customer concerns, offer support, and build relationships in real-time. The fast-food industry, with companies like Domino's Pizza using online ordering and real-time tracking, is a prime illustration of this real-time interaction.

Consumer Empowerment: In the digital age, consumers have become more empowered than ever before. They have access to an abundance of information and can research products and services before making decisions. Businesses that provide transparent information and value-driven content gain the trust of their audience. TripAdvisor, for instance, empowers travellers by offering reviews and ratings, influencing their choices.

Cost-Effective Marketing: Traditional advertising methods often require significant financial investment. In contrast, digital advertising offers a cost-effective way for businesses to promote their products or services. Social media platforms, such as Facebook and Instagram, enable targeted ad campaigns that reach specific demographics at a fraction of the cost of traditional advertising.

Global Community Building: The digital revolution has paved the way for businesses to build communities around their brands. Companies like Apple have created a global community of enthusiasts and advocates who connect, share experiences, and even co-create content. This sense of belonging strengthens brand loyalty and fosters organic growth.

The digital revolution's significance goes beyond businesses. For consumers, it means more choice, greater convenience, and a voice in shaping the products and services they use. The convenience of online shopping, the power to influence brands, and access to a world of information are just a few of the benefits enjoyed by consumers today.

In "The Digital Revolution: Why it Matters," we unravel the profound impact of this transformation and provide real-world examples that illustrate how businesses and consumers have benefited from the digital shift. Understanding this significance is the first step towards harnessing the full potential of digital advertising to achieve your business goals and meet the evolving needs of your audience.

Objectives of the eBook

As we embark on this journey, it's crucial to establish the goals of this eBook. Here, we outline the objectives and benefits you can expect from reading this comprehensive guide. You'll discover how this eBook will equip you with the knowledge and tools needed to leverage digital advertising effectively, whether you're a business owner looking to expand your reach or a marketer seeking to enhance your skills.

With a clear understanding of the evolution of advertising, the importance of the digital revolution, and the objectives of this eBook, you'll be well-prepared to explore the exciting world of digital advertising and its potential for growing your business.

Chapter 2: The Fundamentals of Digital Advertising

In this chapter, we will lay the foundation for your journey into digital advertising. Understanding the fundamentals is essential to harness the power of this versatile and dynamic marketing medium.

Defining Digital Advertising

Digital advertising refers to the promotion of products, services, or brands through digital channels. Unlike traditional advertising, which primarily relies on print, TV, or radio, digital advertising leverages the internet and electronic devices. This can include various formats such as text, images, videos, and interactive content, strategically placed across digital platforms to reach and engage your target audience.

Key Terminology: Impressions, Clicks, CTR, CPC, CPM, CPA

To navigate the digital advertising landscape effectively, you must familiarize yourself with the key terminology. Here are some essential terms to get you started:

- Impressions: The number of times your ad is displayed on a user's screen. Impressions are a measure of your ad's visibility.
- Clicks: The number of times users click on your ad. Clicks indicate the level of interest your ad generates.
- CTR (Click-Through Rate): CTR is calculated by dividing the number of clicks by the number of impressions and is expressed as a percentage. It measures how effective your ad is at encouraging users to act.
- CPC (Cost Per Click): The cost you pay for each click on your ad. It's a common pricing model in digital advertising, especially in platforms like Google Ads.
- CPM (Cost Per Mille): CPM represents the cost for 1,000 ad impressions. It's often used in display and social media advertising campaigns.
- CPA (Cost Per Acquisition): CPA measures the cost of acquiring a new customer or lead through your ad. It's a crucial metric for understanding your return on investment.

Understanding these terms is pivotal as you monitor, measure, and optimize your digital advertising campaigns. They provide insights into the performance of your ads and help you make informed decisions to improve results.

Benefits of Digital Advertising

Digital advertising offers a plethora of advantages that make it a preferred choice for businesses of all sizes. Here are some key benefits:

1. Precise Targeting: Digital advertising allows you to reach a particular audience based on demographics, interests, behaviour, and more. This precision helps you connect with the right people at the right time.
2. Cost-Effectiveness: Compared to traditional advertising, digital advertising often provides a better return on investment. You can set budgets, and many platforms offer flexible pricing models, ensuring you get the most value for your money.

3. Real-Time Results: With digital advertising, you don't have to wait for weeks or months to see the impact of your campaigns. Real-time data and analytics enable you to adjust on the fly for improved results.
4. Detailed Audience Insights: Digital platforms offer rich data and analytics, giving you a deep understanding of your audience's behaviour. This information is invaluable for refining your advertising strategies.
5. Immediate Feedback and Optimization: You can quickly assess the performance of your ads and make adjustments based on the data. This agility is essential for staying competitive in a fast-paced digital world.

As we delve deeper into this ebook, you'll explore the various platforms available and how to create effective ad campaigns. But mastering the fundamentals is the first step in your journey to digital advertising success.

Chapter 3: Platforms for Digital Advertising

In the vast world of digital advertising, various platforms provide opportunities to reach your target audience effectively. This chapter delves into the key platforms that you can leverage to grow your business.

- **Search Engine Marketing (SEM)**

  Search Engine Marketing, often referred to as SEM, is a powerhouse in the digital advertising realm. It allows you to place ads within search engine results, ensuring your brand is visible to potential customers actively looking for products or services.

- **Google Ads**

  Google Ads, formerly known as Google AdWords, is the go-to platform for SEM. With its powerful reach and extensive ad formats, it enables you to connect with a global audience and tailor your ads to match user intent.

- **Bing Ads**

  While Google dominates the search engine market, Bing Ads should not be overlooked. It offers a distinct user base and can be a cost-effective option, especially for niche markets.

- **Social Media Advertising**

  Social media platforms have become a central hub for connecting with audiences, and they offer diverse advertising options to suit different businesses.

- **Facebook Advertising**

  With its immense user base, Facebook Advertising is a versatile platform to target demographics, interests, and behaviors. It offers various ad formats, making it suitable for different marketing objectives.

- **Instagram Advertising**

  Instagram's visually appealing platform is ideal for businesses with a strong visual component. You can reach a younger, engaged audience through images and video ads.

- **Twitter Ads**

  Twitter's fast-paced environment is great for real-time engagement and trends. Twitter Ads enable you to join relevant conversations and promote your brand effectively.

- **LinkedIn Advertising**

  LinkedIn caters to a professional audience, making it an excellent choice for B2B marketing. You can target users based on their job titles, industry, and more.

- **Display Advertising**

  Display ads are visual advertisements placed on websites, apps, or social media platforms. They can be in various formats like banners, interactive ads, or video.

- **Video Advertising**

  Video ads have gained immense popularity. Platforms like YouTube and others provide opportunities to showcase your brand through engaging videos.

- **Email Marketing**

  Email marketing is a direct communication channel with your audience. Crafting targeted email campaigns can yield excellent results.

- **Affiliate Marketing**

  Affiliate marketing involves partnering with affiliates who promote your products or services in exchange for a commission. It's a performance-based advertising model.

- **Content Marketing**

  Content marketing involves creating valuable and informative content to attract and engage your audience. It's a subtler, but highly effective form of digital advertising.

Understanding the strengths and weaknesses of these advertising platforms is essential to make informed decisions about where to allocate your resources and efforts. Each platform caters to different goals and target audiences, so choosing the right mix can significantly impact your digital advertising success.

Chapter 4: Targeting and Audience Segmentation

In Chapter 4 of "Digital Advertising Demystified," we delve into the art of targeting and audience segmentation, revealing the strategies and techniques that will make your digital advertising campaigns truly effective.

- **The Power of Targeted Advertising**

  One of the key advantages of digital advertising is its ability to deliver messages directly to your intended audience. In this section, we'll explore the immense power of targeted advertising. No longer do you need to cast a wide net and hope for the best; digital advertising allows you to pinpoint your ideal customers with precision.

- **Demographics, Psychographics, and Behavioral Targeting**

  Understanding your audience is the first step in creating highly effective ad campaigns. We'll guide you through three essential approaches to audience segmentation:

  - Demographics: Learn how to categorize your audience based on age, gender, location, income, and other key demographic factors. This information is fundamental to creating ads that resonate with your target market.
  - Psychographics: Dive deep into the psychological aspects of your audience. What are their interests, values, attitudes, and lifestyle choices? Uncover the power of psychographics in crafting compelling ad messaging.
  - Behavioral Targeting: Explore the fascinating world of behavioral targeting, where you can track user behavior and tailor your ads based on their online activities. This section will teach you how to reach your audience based on their online behavior, such as their browsing history and previous interactions with your website.
  - Retargeting and Remarketing: Ever wondered why that product you recently viewed online seems to follow you around the internet? This is the magic of retargeting and remarketing. In this part of the chapter, we'll demystify these techniques, showing you how to re-engage potential customers who have interacted with your brand or website. We'll discuss the benefits of staying top-of-mind and guide you through setting up your retargeting campaigns.

- **Ad Personalization**

  One-size-fits-all advertising is a thing of the past. Today's consumers expect personalized experiences, and digital advertising can deliver just that. Discover the power of ad personalization in this section. We'll walk you through the process of tailoring your ads to individual preferences, behaviors, and interests. Personalization is the key to making your audience feel valued and understood, ultimately driving higher engagement and conversions.

  In the digital advertising landscape, one size does not fit all. To truly connect with your audience and drive higher engagement and conversions, you need to embrace ad personalization. This approach involves crafting ads that resonate with individual preferences, behaviors, and interests, making each member of your audience feel valued and understood.

Understanding Your Audience

Ad personalization begins with a deep understanding of your target audience. The more you know about them, the better you can tailor your messaging. Here's how to get started:

Data Collection: Gather data on your audience, including demographics, location, and past interactions with your brand.

Behavioral Insights: Analyze how users navigate your website, what products they've viewed, and their purchase history.

User Preferences: Collect information on their interests, such as hobbies, preferences, and values.

Creating Personalized Ads

Once you've collected the necessary data, it's time to put it to use in crafting personalized ads. Here are some strategies to implement:

Dynamic Ads: These ads automatically change content based on user behavior. For instance, an e-commerce site might show products related to what a user recently viewed.

Recommendation Engines: Like what you see on Amazon, these systems suggest products or content based on a user's history and preferences.

Geo-Targeting: Tailor ads based on a user's location. For instance, a restaurant chain can show different specials based on the nearest location.

Personalized Email Campaigns: Craft email content that speaks directly to a user's past interactions. For example, if a user abandoned a shopping cart, send a reminder email with the items they left behind.

Examples of Successful Ad Personalization

Amazon: The e-commerce giant excels at ad personalization. It recommends products based on your browsing and purchase history, making you feel like it knows your preferences.

Spotify: This music streaming platform curates personalized playlists for each user based on their listening habits, creating a unique listening experience.

Netflix: The streaming service customizes content recommendations, cover images, and even episode orders based on your viewing history.

Airbnb: By showing properties based on your location, past bookings, and travel interests, Airbnb offers a highly personalized experience.

The Benefits of Ad Personalization

Higher Engagement: When users feel that the content is relevant to them, they're more likely to interact with your ads.

Increased Conversions: Tailored messaging increases the chances of users taking desired actions, such as making a purchase or signing up.

Customer Loyalty: Personalization can foster a sense of loyalty as users appreciate the effort to cater to their needs.

Ad personalization is the key to forging stronger connections with your audience and ensuring that your digital advertising efforts are not only effective but also appreciated. Remember that respecting user privacy and providing value are essential components of a successful personalization strategy.

These strategies are the cornerstone of crafting ad campaigns that resonate with your audience and drive real results. With the insights provided in this chapter, you'll be well on your way to becoming a digital advertising expert.

Chapter 5: Creating Effective Ad Campaigns

In the world of digital advertising, success hinges on creating ad campaigns that resonate with your target audience. To achieve this, you'll need to master various aspects, from setting clear goals and objectives to crafting compelling ad creatives. In this chapter, we'll explore the key elements that make up an effective ad campaign.

Creating effective ad campaigns is a skill that can transform your digital advertising efforts into a powerhouse of results. By the end of this chapter, you'll be equipped with the knowledge and strategies to set clear objectives, design captivating ad creatives, write persuasive ad copy, optimize landing pages, and harness the power of A/B testing and analytics. It's time to take your digital advertising game to the next level and achieve your business objectives with confidence.

- **Setting Clear Goals and Objectives**

  Your journey in digital advertising begins with a well-defined destination. Setting clear goals and objectives is the foundational step to any successful campaign. Without a roadmap, you risk wandering aimlessly in the vast digital landscape. Whether it's increasing brand awareness, boosting website traffic, or driving conversions, your objectives should be specific, measurable, achievable, relevant, and time-bound (SMART).

- **Ad Design and Creatives**

  Visual appeal is the first hook that grabs your audience's attention. The ad design and creatives play a pivotal role in conveying your message and creating a lasting impression. We'll delve into the principles of effective design, the use of eye-catching visuals, and how to maintain brand consistency. Learn how to choose the right imagery, colors, and typography that align with your brand and campaign goals.

  Principles of Effective Design:

  Simplicity: Keep your ad design clean and uncluttered. Avoid overwhelming your audience with too much information or visual elements.

  Clarity: Ensure that your message is crystal clear. Use straightforward language and visuals that directly convey your intended message.

  Visual Hierarchy: Organize the elements of your ad so that the most important information is the most prominent. Use size, color, and placement to guide the viewer's eye.

  Consistency: Maintain a consistent design across all your ads to reinforce brand identity and recognition.

  Balance: Distribute elements evenly to create a sense of balance and harmony in your ad.

  Contrast: Use contrasting colors and typography to highlight key elements and make them stand out.

  Whitespace: Embrace whitespace to create a sense of elegance and draw attention to your content.

Mobile Responsiveness: Ensure your ad design works seamlessly on all devices, especially mobile, as a significant portion of users access content on smartphones.

Use of Eye-Catching Visuals:

Relevance: Visuals should be relevant to your brand and message. Choose images or graphics that resonate with your target audience.

Emotion: Select visuals that evoke the desired emotions or feelings that align with your campaign's goals. Emotional connection can be a powerful tool.

Quality: Use high-quality, professional images and graphics to maintain a polished appearance.

Originality: If possible, use original visuals that set you apart from the competition and showcase your unique brand identity.

Consistency: Ensure that the style and tone of your visuals align with your brand's overall visual identity.

Maintaining Brand Consistency:

Color Palette: Define a brand color palette and stick to it. Use these colors consistently in your ad designs to reinforce brand recognition.

Typography: Choose a set of fonts that represent your brand's personality. Consistency in font choices across all materials is essential.

Logo Usage: Integrate your logo into your ad designs while ensuring it doesn't overshadow the core message.

Imagery Style: Maintain a consistent style of imagery, whether it's photography, illustrations, or graphics, that complements your brand.

Messaging: Ensure that the voice and tone of your ad copy align with your brand's overall communication style.

Layouts: Stick to a consistent layout format that your audience can recognize as your brand's signature style.

Choosing Imagery, Colors, and Typography:

Imagery: Select imagery that tells a story or conveys an emotion related to your campaign. For example, if you're promoting eco-friendly products, use images of nature or sustainable living. If you're advertising tech gadgets, opt for sleek, modern visuals.

Colors: Choose colors that represent your brand values and resonate with your target audience. For instance, blue conveys trust and professionalism, while green symbolizes nature and sustainability.

Typography: Use fonts that match your brand personality. Playful brands might opt for whimsical fonts, while serious, corporate brands would lean towards more traditional, serif fonts.

Example 1 - Car Advertisement:

Design: Sleek, modern, with a focus on the car's curves and features.
Colors: Metallic grays and blues to convey a sense of sophistication.
Typography: Clean, sans-serif fonts for a high-tech, modern feel.

Example 2 - Eco-Friendly Product Promotion:

Design: Bright and vibrant imagery showcasing the product's environmental benefits.
Colors: Earthy greens and blues to emphasize sustainability and nature.
Typography: Friendly and approachable fonts for a warm and welcoming vibe.

Example 3 - Luxury Fashion Ad:

Design: High-quality, elegant visuals that highlight the fashion items.
Colors: Rich, deep colors like black, gold, and deep reds for a luxurious touch.
Typography: Serif fonts for a sense of tradition and sophistication.

By following these principles and considering these examples, you can create ad designs and creatives that effectively convey your brand's message, connect with your audience, and achieve your campaign goals.

- **Ad Copywriting Tips**

  Words are powerful tools in digital advertising. Crafting compelling ad copy is an art that combines creativity with persuasion. We'll provide you with essential ad copywriting tips to help you write captivating headlines and persuasive ad text. Discover techniques to evoke emotions, highlight benefits, and create a sense of urgency that drives action.

  Craft a Captivating Headline:

  Your headline is the first thing readers see. Make it attention-grabbing and relevant. Use action words, numbers, and questions.
  Example: "Get 50% Off Your Next Adventure!"

  Understand Your Audience:

  Tailor your ad to your target audience. Use language, tone, and style that resonates with them.
  Example: "Discover the Perfect Skincare Solution for Sensitive Skin."

  Highlight Benefits, Not Features:

  Focus on how your product or service solves a problem or fulfills a need. Emphasize the benefits for the customer.
  Example: "Save Time and Money with Our Quick and Affordable Home Cleaning Service."

Create a Sense of Urgency:

Encourage immediate action with phrases like "Limited Time Offer" or "Act Now." Highlight scarcity.
Example: "Last Chance to Buy! Sale Ends Tomorrow."

Use Persuasive Language:

Employ power words like "exclusive," "guaranteed," or "free" to make your offer more enticing.
Example: "Unlock Exclusive Access to Our Premium Content."

Keep It Concise:

Get to the point quickly. Avoid unnecessary jargon. Brevity is key in digital advertising.
Example: "Revamp Your Style with Our New Collection."

Tell a Compelling Story:

Connect with your audience emotionally by sharing a relatable story or testimonial.
Example: "Meet Sarah: How Our Fitness Program Transformed Her Life."

Evoke Emotions:

Appeal to your audience's emotions, whether it's excitement, fear, joy, or nostalgia. Stir emotions with your ad copy.
Example: "Experience the Thrill of Adventure with Our Exciting Travel Packages."

Effective Design Principles

Simplicity is Key:

Keep your ad clean and uncluttered. A simple design makes it easier for the audience to focus on your message.

Consistent Branding:

Maintain a cohesive look with your brand's colors, fonts, and logo. Consistency builds recognition.

Eye-Catching Visuals:

Use high-quality, relevant images or videos that enhance your message. Visuals should support the ad's purpose.

Readable Typography:

Choose legible fonts and text sizes. Make sure the text is easily readable on all devices.

Whitespace:

Don't overcrowd the ad with content. Allow for ample whitespace to guide the reader's attention.

Call-to-Action (CTA) Button:

Make your CTA button prominent, with contrasting colors and clear text. Use action-oriented phrases like "Buy Now" or "Learn More."

Mobile Optimization:

Ensure your ad is responsive and looks great on mobile devices. Most users access digital content on smartphones.

By incorporating these ad copywriting tips and effective design principles, you can create persuasive and visually appealing advertisements that resonate with your audience, drive action, and deliver impactful results in the world of digital advertising.

- **Landing Page Optimization**

  Your ad campaign may grab attention, but it's your landing page that seals the deal. Learn how to create landing pages that are congruent with your ads and designed for conversion. We'll cover best practices in layout, content, and call-to-action buttons to keep visitors engaged and guide them toward the desired action.

  Layout:

  Clean and Uncluttered Design: Ensure that the landing page is visually clean, uncluttered, and easy to navigate. Avoid distracting elements that may divert visitors' attention.
  Mobile Responsiveness: Make sure your landing page is mobile-friendly as many users access content on smartphones. Test the layout on various devices to ensure a seamless experience.
  Logical Flow: Organize the content logically, guiding visitors from the headline to the call to action (CTA) in a natural progression.
  Whitespace: Use ample whitespace to give breathing room to text and visuals. It makes the page more visually appealing and easier to read.
  High-Quality Imagery: Include relevant, high-resolution images and graphics that support the content and reinforce the message.

  Content:

  Compelling Headline: Craft a clear and attention-grabbing headline that communicates the value or benefit the visitor will receive.
  Example: "Unlock the Secrets to Digital Advertising Success."

Informative Subheading: Use a subheading to provide additional context or a brief summary of what the landing page offers.
Example: "Learn how to optimize landing pages for higher conversions."

Engaging Copy: Write concise and persuasive copy that addresses the visitor's pain points and offers solutions.
Example: "Discover proven techniques to make your landing pages work for you."

Bullet Points: Use bullet points to highlight key benefits or features. They make information scannable and digestible.
Example:

Increase conversion rates
Boost user engagement
Maximize ROI

Social Proof: Include testimonials, reviews, or case studies that build trust and credibility.

Example: "Read how Company XYZ achieved a 200% increase in conversions using our landing page optimization strategies."

Call-to-Action Buttons:

Clear and Action-Oriented: The CTA button should have clear and action-oriented text that tells the visitor what to do next.
Example: "Get Started," "Download Now," "Sign Up," "Request a Free Consultation."

Contrasting Color: Use a color that contrasts with the overall page design, making the button stand out.

Placement: Position the CTA prominently, preferably above the fold (visible without scrolling), and at the end of a section with persuasive content.

Size: Ensure the button is of an adequate size that's easy to tap or click on both desktop and mobile devices.

Whitespace Around CTA: Leave whitespace around the CTA button to draw attention to it and make it easily clickable.

Limited Options: Avoid too many CTAs on the same page; focus on the primary action you want visitors to take.

Example CTA:

Text: "Download Our Ebook"
Color: Vibrant orange
Placement: Positioned above the fold after explaining the ebook's value
Size: Large enough to catch the eye but not overwhelming
Whitespace: Sufficient space around the CTA to make it stand out

By implementing these best practices, your Landing Page will effectively engage visitors and guide them toward the desired action, which in this case is likely to download or access your ebook.

- **A/B Testing and Analytics**

  The digital advertising landscape is dynamic, and what works today may not work tomorrow. That's where A/B testing and analytics come into play. Explore the power of experimentation and optimization by testing different ad variations. We'll guide you through setting up tests, measuring performance, and making data-driven decisions to enhance your campaigns continuously.

  In the world of digital advertising, data is your North Star. Without data-driven insights, you're navigating blind. The ability to test, measure, and make informed decisions is a superpower for advertisers. This chapter will guide you through A/B testing and analytics, showing you how to enhance your campaigns continuously.

Setting up A/B Tests

Step 1: Define Your Goals and Hypotheses

Before you start testing, be crystal clear about what you want to achieve. Are you testing a new ad copy, a different color scheme, or a changed call-to-action? Once you have your goals, formulate hypotheses. For example, "Changing the headline from 'Get Fit Today' to 'Transform Your Life' will increase click-through rates."

Step 2: Create Variations

Design different versions of your ad, webpage, or email. The original is your control (A), and the altered version is your variation (B).

Step 3: Randomize and Split

Randomly show the control or variation to your audience. Split testing tools do this automatically to ensure fairness.

Step 4: Run the Test

Let your A/B test run for a set period or until you've gathered enough data (typically a few weeks). Ensure that the variables being tested are the only ones that change during this period.

Measuring Performance

Step 5: Collect Data

Monitor the performance of your A and B versions. Track metrics like CTR, conversion rate, bounce rate, and revenue generated.

Step 6: Analyze Results

Use statistical analysis to determine which version performed better. Pay attention to significance levels; a higher sample size usually means more reliable results.

Step 7: Draw Conclusions

If your variation outperforms the control, it's time to draw conclusions. Did your hypothesis hold true? If the control performs better, what can you learn from the variation's shortcomings?

Making Data-Driven Decisions

Step 8: Implement Changes

If your variation wins, implement the changes throughout your campaign. If it loses, analyze what didn't work and use these insights to fine-tune your next test.

Step 9: Continuous Improvement

A/B testing should be an ongoing process. Continuously refine your campaigns. Test various elements, monitor performance, and iterate. Over time, this will lead to higher-performing ads and campaigns.

Examples:

Example 1 - Testing Ad Copy

Goal: Increase click-through rates (CTR) for an online fitness program.

Hypothesis: Changing the ad headline from "Get Fit Today" to "Transform Your Life" will increase CTR.

A (Control): "Get Fit Today"
B (Variation): "Transform Your Life"

After a 4-week A/B test, the results show that the variation with "Transform Your Life" increased CTR by 12%. The hypothesis proved correct.

Example 2 - Landing Page Layout

Goal: Improve the conversion rate on a product page.

Hypothesis: Changing the product image's placement will increase the conversion rate.

A (Control): Product image on the left
B (Variation): Product image on the right

After a 3-week A/B test, the results indicate that the variation with the product image on the right increased the conversion rate by 8%.

A/B testing, coupled with data-driven decision-making, empowers you to optimize your digital advertising campaigns continually. It's a journey of improvement, allowing you to make strategic changes based on what resonates most with your audience, ultimately leading to more effective and successful campaigns.

Creating effective ad campaigns is a skill that can transform your digital advertising efforts into a powerhouse of results. By the end of this chapter, you'll be equipped with the knowledge and strategies to set clear objectives, design captivating ad creatives, write persuasive ad copy, optimize landing pages, and harness the power of A/B testing and analytics. It's time to take your digital advertising game to the next level and achieve your business objectives with confidence.

Chapter 6: Measuring and Analyzing Performance

In the world of digital advertising, the key to success lies in data. In Chapter 6, we'll explore the critical aspects of measuring and analyzing performance to ensure your campaigns deliver the best results.

We'll equip you with the skills to not only measure and analyze the performance of your digital advertising campaigns but also to make data-driven decisions that will boost the success of your future endeavors. This knowledge is a pivotal step towards mastering the digital advertising landscape and achieving your business objectives.

- **Key Performance Indicators (KPIs)**
  Every successful digital advertising campaign starts with well-defined Key Performance Indicators (KPIs). These are the metrics that allow you to track and evaluate the effectiveness of your ads. We'll delve into the most common KPIs, such as click-through rate (CTR), conversion rate, return on investment (ROI), and more. Understanding these KPIs is essential for setting clear objectives and measuring the impact of your efforts.

- **Google Analytics and Other Tracking Tools**
  To monitor your campaigns effectively, you need the right tools. Google Analytics is a powerhouse in the digital advertising world. We'll guide you through setting up Google Analytics and using its various features to gain valuable insights into user behavior, demographics, and much more. Additionally, we'll introduce you to other tracking tools and their benefits, giving you a well-rounded view of your ad performance.

Google Analytics: Unveiling User Insights

Google Analytics is a powerful tool that provides a treasure trove of information about how users interact with your website. Here's a step-by-step guide to setting up and using Google Analytics:

Step 1: Account Creation

Sign up for a Google Analytics account using your Google account credentials.
Create a new property for your website, which will generate a unique tracking code.

Step 2: Installing the Tracking Code

Copy the tracking code and paste it into the HTML of your website's pages, typically just before the closing </head> tag.

Step 3: Understanding the Dashboard

Explore the Google Analytics dashboard, which provides an overview of your website's performance.
Get familiar with metrics like sessions, users, bounce rate, and average session duration.

Step 4: Audience Insights

Dive into the "Audience" section to learn more about your visitors.
Discover demographics (age, gender), interests, and geographic locations of your users.

Step 5: Behavior Analysis

Check out the "Behavior" section to understand how users navigate your site.
Track page views, average time on page, and user flow through your website.

Step 6: Acquisition and Conversions

Examine the "Acquisition" section to see where your traffic is coming from (e.g., organic search, social media, referrals).
Track conversion goals, such as form submissions or e-commerce transactions.

Step 7: Real-Time Monitoring

Use the "Real-Time" feature to see live data on current website activity.
Monitor how your audience interacts with your site in real-time.

Step 8: Custom Reports and Alerts

Create custom reports and set up email alerts for specific metrics you want to track.

Other Tracking Tools: Expanding Your Insights

While Google Analytics is a fantastic tool, it's not the only one available. Other tracking tools can complement your data analysis efforts. Here are a few worth considering:

Hotjar: Hotjar offers heatmaps, session recordings, and user surveys to help you understand how visitors interact with your site.

Moz Pro: A comprehensive SEO toolset that provides valuable insights into your website's performance in search engine rankings.

Kissmetrics: Focuses on understanding individual user behavior and customer journeys, helping you optimize your marketing strategies.

Facebook Pixel: A must-have for Facebook advertisers, this tool tracks conversions and allows for precise retargeting.

SEMrush: Offers competitive analysis, keyword research, and backlink tracking to boost your SEO efforts.

By incorporating these tracking tools alongside Google Analytics, you can gain a more comprehensive view of your ad performance, user behavior, and audience demographics. Each tool brings its unique strengths and features to the table, enabling you to fine-tune your digital advertising strategy for optimal results.

- **Interpreting Data**

Collecting data is one thing; interpreting it is another. In this section, we'll show you how to make sense of the numbers and graphs. You'll learn to recognize patterns, identify areas of improvement, and spot trends that can guide your future advertising strategies. Our goal is to empower you to turn raw data into actionable insights.

Understanding the numbers and graphs generated by your digital advertising campaigns is essential for making informed decisions and optimizing your strategies. In this section, we'll explore key metrics and provide examples to help you interpret the data effectively.

Key Metrics for Data Interpretation

Click-Through Rate (CTR): This metric reveals the effectiveness of your ad in enticing users to click. A higher CTR indicates a more compelling ad. For example, if your ad receives 100 clicks from 1,000 impressions, your CTR is 10%.

Conversion Rate: Measure the percentage of users who completed a desired action, like making a purchase. If 50 out of 1,000 visitors made a purchase, your conversion rate is 5%.

Cost Per Click (CPC): Understand how much you pay for each click. If you spent $200 on an ad campaign that generated 100 clicks, your CPC is $2.

Cost Per Acquisition (CPA): This metric calculates the cost to acquire a customer. If your campaign cost $500 and led to 50 conversions, your CPA is $10.

Bounce Rate: This metric tells you the percentage of users who leave your website after viewing only one page. A high bounce rate could indicate a need for better landing page optimization.

Return on Investment (ROI): ROI measures the profitability of your advertising efforts. If you spent $1,000 on an ad campaign and generated $2,000 in revenue, your ROI is 100%.

Ad Position: Consider the placement of your ads on search engine results pages. Higher positions can lead to increased visibility and clicks.

Interpreting Data for Optimization

Example 1: CTR Analysis

Let's say you have two ads running, Ad A and Ad B. Ad A has a CTR of 3%, and Ad B has a CTR of 8%. It's clear that Ad B is more effective in engaging your audience, so you might want to allocate more budget to it or analyze what elements make it successful.

Example 2: Conversion Rate Evaluation

You're running an email marketing campaign, and you notice that one email variant has a conversion rate of 10%, while another has a rate of 5%. By comparing their content, design, and subject lines, you can identify what elements make the high-converting email effective and apply those insights to future campaigns.

Example 3: Bounce Rate Reduction

Your website has a high bounce rate of 70%. Upon reviewing the analytics, you notice that the majority of users leave from a specific landing page. By improving the content, design, or call-to-action on that page, you can reduce the bounce rate and keep visitors engaged.

Example 4: ROI Assessment

You've run two advertising campaigns with similar budgets. The first campaign generated $3,000 in revenue, resulting in an ROI of 150%, while the second campaign brought in $1,000 and had an ROI of 50%. It's clear that the first campaign is more profitable, indicating where you should focus your efforts and budget.

By mastering these key metrics and interpreting data effectively, you can identify patterns, areas of improvement, and trends that will guide your future advertising strategies. The ability to turn raw data into actionable insights is a powerful skill that will drive your digital advertising success.

- **Adjusting Campaigns Based on Data**

  Data analysis is just the beginning; acting based on your findings is where the real transformation happens. We'll discuss the art of adjusting your campaigns in real time. You'll discover how to optimize ad creatives, adjust targeting parameters, and make budget allocations that align with your goals. By adapting your campaigns based on data, you'll continuously improve your advertising ROI.

  One of the defining features of digital advertising is the ability to make real-time adjustments to your ad campaigns based on data. This flexibility is a game-changer, allowing you to optimize your advertising strategy continuously. In this section, we'll delve into the art of fine-tuning your campaigns using data-driven insights, with practical examples to illustrate the process.

1. Monitor Key Performance Indicators (KPIs):

Example: Let's say you're running a Facebook ad campaign for your e-commerce store. You notice a high click-through rate (CTR) but a low conversion rate. By monitoring these KPIs, you realize that the ad is attracting clicks but failing to convert visitors into customers.

2. Ad Creatives and Copy Adjustments:

Example: You're running a Google Ads campaign for your software product. You experiment with different ad headlines and descriptions. After a week, you notice that one version has a significantly higher click-through rate. By adapting your ad creatives based on this data, you can attract more clicks.

3. Targeting Parameters Optimization:

Example: Suppose you're advertising a luxury travel service. Your initial campaign targets users interested in travel. However, by examining data, you discover that users with higher incomes are converting at a much higher rate. You adjust your targeting to focus on this affluent demographic.

4. Ad Scheduling and Budget Allocation:

Example: Your online clothing store is running a paid search campaign on Google. Data analysis reveals that your ads perform better during weekdays and specific hours. You allocate a higher budget to those peak times and days, ensuring you maximize your ad spend.

5. Geographic Adjustments:

Example: You're promoting your local coffee shop using geotargeted Facebook ads. Data shows that the majority of your conversions come from users within a 5-mile radius. You refine your targeting to concentrate your ad delivery within this radius for a more efficient campaign.

6. Ad Placement Optimization:

Example: You're running a display ad campaign for your fitness app. Data reveals that your ads perform exceptionally well on health and fitness websites but poorly on unrelated sites. You adjust your campaign to focus exclusively on websites related to health and fitness.

7. A/B Testing and Iteration:

Example: You're advertising your new line of smartphones with two different landing page designs. By A/B testing, you discover that version B has a significantly higher conversion rate. You stop the campaign for version A and allocate the budget to version B for better results.

8. Negative Keywords and Exclusions:

Example: Your online pet store is running a Google Ads campaign for dog-related products. Data reveals that clicks for "cat food" keywords are draining your budget without yielding conversions. You add "cat food" as a negative keyword to prevent such clicks.

9. Ad Format and Placement:

Example: You're using Instagram ads to promote your fashion brand. Data shows that carousel ads outperform image ads, and mobile placement is more effective than desktop. You adjust your ad format and placement to capitalize on this information.

10. Review and Iterate:

Example: Over time, you notice that your social media ads receive more engagement and conversions during certain seasons. You create a content calendar to align your campaigns with these peak periods, ensuring a more consistent return on investment.

By continuously adjusting your campaigns based on data, you're not only saving precious ad budget but also increasing the effectiveness of your advertising. The key is to stay vigilant, test hypotheses, and be ready to adapt to changing circumstances. Your advertising efforts will become more efficient and results-driven, ultimately boosting your ROI and helping your business grow.

Chapter 7: Why Digital Advertising Works

In the ever-expanding world of digital advertising, understanding why it works can be the key to unlocking your business's full potential. In this chapter, we'll explore six key reasons why digital advertising is not just effective but essential for your growth.

- **Reach and Scalability**

  One of the most compelling aspects of digital advertising is its unparalleled reach. With the power of the internet, you can connect with potential customers around the world. Whether you're targeting a local market or a global audience, digital advertising ensures your message reaches the right eyes and ears. The scalability of digital advertising allows you to adjust your budget and campaign size as your business grows, ensuring your reach evolves with you.

- **Cost-Effectiveness**

  Traditional advertising methods often come with hefty price tags, making it challenging for small businesses to compete. Digital advertising levels the playing field. With flexible budgets and a range of cost models, such as Pay-Per-Click (PPC) and Cost-Per-Mille (CPM), you have precise control over your spending. This cost-effectiveness allows businesses of all sizes to advertise within their means, making every dollar count.

- **Real-Time Results**

  Imagine running a television ad campaign and waiting weeks for viewership data. With digital advertising, you don't have to. The real-time nature of digital platforms provides immediate feedback on how your ads are performing. From click-through rates to conversion statistics, you can adapt and optimize your strategy on the fly, ensuring you get the best results in real-time.

- **Detailed Audience Insights**

  In the digital world, data is king. Digital advertising platforms provide a treasure trove of audience insights. You can access information about your audience's demographics, interests, online behavior, and more. This wealth of data enables you to create highly targeted and personalized ad campaigns, ensuring your message resonates with the right people at the right time.

- **Immediate Feedback and Optimization**

  Digital advertising is not a one-and-done process. It's a dynamic, ever-evolving strategy. The immediate feedback provided by digital platforms allows you to make data-driven decisions swiftly. If an ad isn't performing as expected, you can adjust it or allocate your budget differently. This adaptability and agility ensure your advertising efforts remain effective.

- **Case Studies: Success Stories**

  To further illustrate why digital advertising works, we've included real-world case studies. These success stories demonstrate how businesses, large and small, have leveraged digital advertising to achieve remarkable results. You'll learn from their experiences and gain valuable insights into the diverse ways digital advertising can drive business growth.

- o Airbnb's Instagram Story Ads: Airbnb used Instagram Story ads to promote unique accommodations. By targeting users with a passion for travel and adventure, they achieved a 13-point lift in ad recall. This case highlights the power of social media advertising in reaching a highly engaged audience.
- o Dollar Shave Club's Viral Video: Dollar Shave Club's humorous video ad went viral on YouTube. The ad's creative approach and storytelling led to massive brand exposure, rapid customer acquisition, and a successful subscription model. It illustrates how video advertising can capture attention and drive growth.

- o Coca-Cola's Personalized Email Campaign: Coca-Cola implemented a highly personalized email campaign, addressing customers by name and recommending products based on their previous purchases. This led to a significant increase in click-through rates and conversions, demonstrating the impact of email marketing.

- o Amazon's Remarketing Strategy: Amazon is a master of remarketing. They retarget users with personalized product recommendations based on their previous searches and purchases. This strategy has significantly increased sales and showcases the importance of retargeting.

- o HubSpot's Content Marketing: HubSpot used content marketing to create a vast library of valuable resources, including blog posts, e-books, and webinars. By offering high-quality, educational content, they attracted and nurtured leads, leading to substantial business growth.

- o Geico's SEM Success: Geico effectively utilizes search engine marketing (SEM). They bid on keywords related to insurance, ensuring their ads appear prominently in search results. This strategy has consistently increased website traffic and conversions.

- o Nike's Social Media Advertising: Nike's social media campaigns, particularly on platforms like Instagram and Twitter, have been highly successful. By aligning their brand with athletes and sporting events, they've built a strong, engaged community and increased sales.

These case studies offer valuable insights into the diverse approaches to digital advertising. Readers can learn from the experiences of these successful businesses and adapt strategies to their own campaigns, whether that's through compelling video ads, personalized email marketing, content creation, effective SEM, or strategic use of social media platforms. The key takeaway is that digital advertising offers numerous avenues for growth, and creativity and audience targeting are often the driving forces behind success.

In this chapter, we've explored the core reasons why digital advertising stands out as the go-to medium for reaching your audience. Its unparalleled reach, cost-effectiveness, real-time results, detailed audience insights, immediate feedback, and a collection of success stories all contribute to its effectiveness. By understanding and harnessing these advantages, you can propel your business to new heights in the digital age.

Chapter 8: Navigating the Changing Digital Landscape

The digital landscape is in a constant state of flux, driven by advancements in technology and changing user behaviors. To stay ahead of the game and continue to grow your business, you must be prepared to navigate this evolving terrain. In this chapter, we'll explore several key factors that are shaping the future of digital advertising.

- **The Impact of Emerging Technologies (AI, AR, VR)**

  Artificial Intelligence (AI), Augmented Reality (AR), and Virtual Reality (VR) are not just buzzwords; they are transformative forces in the digital advertising world. AI enables smart data analysis, personalization, and automation, making your ad campaigns more efficient and effective. AR and VR provide immersive experiences that can captivate your audience. Learn how to harness these technologies to create engaging ads and deliver unique user experiences.

- **Privacy Concerns and Data Regulations**

  In an age where data privacy is a hot topic, it's crucial to understand the implications of privacy concerns and data regulations. The General Data Protection Regulation (GDPR) and similar laws have reshaped the way businesses collect and handle user data. We'll delve into the importance of compliance, user consent, and transparent data practices to build trust with your audience and avoid legal troubles.

Compliance with Data Regulations:

Digital advertising operates in a landscape shaped by various data protection and privacy regulations, such as GDPR (General Data Protection Regulation) in Europe and CCPA (California Consumer Privacy Act) in the United States. Adhering to these regulations is not merely a legal obligation but a fundamental ethical responsibility. By complying with these laws, you demonstrate your commitment to respecting user privacy and their data rights.

User Consent:

Obtaining user consent is a cornerstone of responsible digital advertising. When users provide explicit consent for data collection and usage, it establishes a transparent and trusting relationship. Consent ensures that users have control over their personal information, allowing them to make informed decisions about how their data is used. Failing to obtain consent not only breaches regulations but erodes user trust, leading to potential legal consequences and a damaged reputation.

Transparent Data Practices:

Transparency is key to building trust in digital advertising. Users want to know what data you collect, why you collect it, and how it will be used. Clearly communicating your data practices through privacy policies, terms and conditions, and easy-to-understand language reassures users and makes them more comfortable engaging with your ads. Transparent data practices also help users feel in control and confident in their interactions with your brand.

Building Trust with Your Audience:

Trust is a valuable currency in digital advertising. When users trust your brand, they are more likely to engage with your ads, provide their information, and even become loyal customers. By emphasizing compliance, user consent, and transparent data practices, you convey that you are a trustworthy and responsible advertiser. This trust can lead to higher conversion rates and customer retention, fostering a positive brand image.

Avoiding Legal Troubles:

Non-compliance with data regulations can result in severe legal consequences, including hefty fines and legal actions. Neglecting user consent and failing to maintain transparent data practices can expose your business to costly litigation. It's not just about adhering to the law; it's about avoiding the financial and reputational damage that legal troubles can bring.

In summary, in the world of digital advertising, compliance with data regulations, obtaining user consent, and maintaining transparent data practices are paramount. They not only demonstrate ethical responsibility but also build trust with your audience. Trust is the foundation of successful digital advertising, and by following these principles, you not only enhance your brand's image but also avoid legal troubles that could otherwise jeopardize your business's future.

- **Ad Blockers and Their Implications**

Ad blockers have become a major challenge for digital advertisers. These tools allow users to block unwanted ads, impacting your campaign's visibility and reach. Discover strategies to work around ad blockers, such as creating non-intrusive, high-quality content that users won't want to block. We'll also discuss how to strike a balance between user experience and effective advertising.

Understanding Ad Blockers

Ad blockers are browser extensions or applications that prevent digital ads from displaying on websites and apps. Users install these tools to improve their browsing experience by reducing distractions and page load times. While this may seem like a hurdle for advertisers, there are ways to adapt and overcome these challenges.

Strategies to Work Around Ad Blockers

Create Non-Intrusive Ads: Users often install ad blockers to avoid intrusive and irrelevant ads. Craft your ads to be respectful of user experience. Focus on creating high-quality, non-intrusive ads that seamlessly blend with the content and provide value to the user.

Native Advertising: Native ads mimic the style and format of the platform they appear on, making them less likely to be blocked. These ads can be engaging and relevant, enhancing the user experience.

Sponsored Content: Invest in sponsored content that offers valuable information or entertainment to the audience. Users are less likely to block content that they find informative or entertaining.

Influencer Marketing: Collaborate with influencers in your niche to promote your products or services. Influencer endorsements can be perceived as more genuine and less intrusive.

Content Marketing: Shift your focus towards content marketing, creating informative and engaging blog posts, videos, and infographics. This type of content provides value to users and can be less susceptible to ad blockers.

Email Marketing: While ad blockers can't prevent email ads, be cautious not to overdo it. Craft engaging email campaigns that provide valuable content alongside promotional material.

Balancing User Experience and Effective Advertising

Transparency: Be upfront about your advertising practices. Let users know that your website relies on advertising revenue to provide free content or services. Transparency can build trust with your audience.

Frequency Capping: Limit the number of times an ad is shown to the same user. Excessive ad frequency can annoy users and drive them to install ad blockers.

Ad Relevance: Ensure that your ads are highly relevant to the content and the user's interests. This relevance can mitigate the annoyance factor and make users more accepting of ads.

Optimize Page Load Times: Slow-loading pages can frustrate users, leading them to block ads. Optimize your website's performance to minimize load times.

Use Acceptable Ads Programs: Some ad blockers participate in "acceptable ads" programs, which allow non-intrusive, well-designed ads to pass through. Consider adhering to these standards.

Retargeting with Care: When using retargeting ads, apply frequency caps and ensure that users aren't bombarded with the same ad repeatedly.

By implementing these strategies and finding the right balance between user experience and effective advertising, you can overcome the challenges posed by ad blockers. Advertisers who adapt to these changing dynamics can still reach their target audience effectively and ethically.

- **Preparing for Future Trends**

The digital advertising landscape is continually evolving, and staying ahead means anticipating future trends. We'll provide insights into what's on the horizon, from the rise of voice search and smart speakers to the dominance of video content. Ephemeral content, e-commerce integration, and sustainability in advertising are also covered, giving you a glimpse into the exciting possibilities and challenges that lie ahead.

By understanding and adapting to these changing dynamics, you'll be well-prepared to navigate the digital landscape of tomorrow, ensuring your digital advertising strategies remain effective and competitive. Don't let emerging technologies, privacy concerns, or ad blockers catch you off guard—stay informed and embrace the future of digital advertising.

Chapter 9: Future of Digital Advertising

The digital advertising landscape is in a constant state of flux, driven by rapid technological advancements and evolving consumer behaviors. In this chapter, we'll peer into the crystal ball and explore the exciting future of digital advertising. Get ready to embrace the trends and innovations that will shape the industry in the years to come.

- **Predictions and Trends**

  The first step in navigating the future of digital advertising is understanding the trends and predictions that experts are making. We'll delve into the exciting developments that are on the horizon, including the increasing influence of artificial intelligence and machine learning, the rise of immersive experiences, and the growing importance of data privacy.

  The world of digital advertising is in a constant state of evolution, driven by technological advancements and shifting consumer behaviors. In this chapter, we'll explore some of the exciting developments on the horizon, including:

  1. **The Increasing Influence of Artificial Intelligence and Machine Learning:**
     Artificial intelligence (AI) and machine learning are poised to revolutionize digital advertising. AI algorithms can analyze vast amounts of data to optimize ad targeting, messaging, and delivery. Machine learning helps marketers understand consumer behavior and tailor content accordingly. Expect to see more AI-powered chatbots, personalization, and predictive analytics, making ads more relevant and engaging.

  2. **The Rise of Immersive Experiences:**
     As consumers seek more engaging content, immersive experiences are taking center stage. Augmented reality (AR) and virtual reality (VR) are being integrated into advertising, allowing users to interact with products and services in a virtual environment. Brands are creating immersive storytelling experiences, enhancing user engagement and brand loyalty.

  3. **The Growing Importance of Data Privacy:**
     Data privacy and security have never been more critical. With increasing scrutiny on how personal data is collected and used, regulations like GDPR and CCPA are changing the digital advertising landscape. Marketers must adapt to ensure they're transparent about data usage, obtain proper consents, and prioritize user privacy to build trust with their audience.

  4. **Voice Search and Smart Speakers:**
     Voice search is gaining traction, with the rise of smart speakers like Amazon Echo and Google Home. Advertisers will need to optimize their content for voice search, creating conversational and concise ad campaigns that align with how users speak their queries.

  5. **Video Dominance:**
     Video content is becoming the king of digital advertising. Platforms like YouTube, TikTok, and Instagram are increasingly popular for video marketing. Businesses should invest in video content to engage audiences effectively.

6. **E-commerce Integration:**
   E-commerce and advertising are converging, with shoppable ads and direct purchasing options on social media platforms. Brands that seamlessly integrate e-commerce with advertising will have a competitive edge.

7. **Ephemeral Content**
   Ephemeral content, such as stories on platforms like Instagram and Snapchat, has captured the fleeting attention of users. We'll delve into the psychology behind ephemeral content, its ephemeral nature, and why it's so effective. Discover how to use this format to connect with your audience and build authentic, real-time relationships.

The Psychology Behind Ephemeral Content

Ephemeral content leverages the psychology of anticipation and curiosity. It taps into the human desire for novelty and the thrill of discovery. When people know that content will vanish soon, they're more inclined to pay attention. The mere fact that it's temporary makes it all the more appealing. This curiosity-driven engagement can be harnessed to build strong connections with your audience.

The Ephemeral Nature of Ephemeral Content

The ephemeral nature of this content format mimics real-life conversations and experiences. In a face-to-face conversation, you can't rewind and replay what was said; it's in the moment, and once it's gone, it's gone. Ephemeral content replicates this ephemerality in the digital space, creating a sense of authenticity and spontaneity.

Why Ephemeral Content is So Effective

Fosters Authenticity: Because it's unpolished and fleeting, ephemeral content feels more authentic and relatable. Your audience sees the real you or your brand, not the highly curated version presented in traditional content.

Real-Time Engagement: Ephemeral content invites real-time engagement. Viewers can react, comment, and ask questions, creating a dynamic and immediate connection.

Sense of Urgency: The countdown clock creates a sense of urgency. Users feel compelled to view the content now, as they won't have a second chance. This urgency drives immediate actions, such as clicking through to a product page or signing up for an event.

FOMO and Community: Ephemeral content fosters a sense of community. Viewers know they're part of an exclusive group who are privy to this content. They don't want to miss out, and this feeling of belonging can be a powerful motivator.

Feedback Loop: Real-time engagement and instant feedback allow you to adapt and respond to your audience's needs and preferences more effectively.

Using Ephemeral Content to Connect with Your Audience

To make the most of ephemeral content:

Showcase Authenticity: Don't strive for perfection. Be genuine, and let your audience see the human side of your brand.

Tell a Story: Create a narrative or share behind-the-scenes moments. Storytelling is a powerful way to engage and connect emotionally.

Promotions and Teasers: Use ephemeral content to tease upcoming product launches, events, or special promotions.

Interactive Content: Polls, quizzes, and Q&A sessions are excellent for fostering interaction.

Consistency: Keep a regular schedule, so your audience knows when to expect your ephemeral content.

In a digital world inundated with permanent content, ephemeral content offers a refreshing change. Its ephemeral nature taps into human psychology, building authentic, real-time relationships with your audience. By embracing this format, you can engage, connect, and create a sense of belonging that traditional advertising often struggles to achieve.

8. **Sustainability in Advertising:**

    With growing environmental concerns, sustainability is making its way into advertising. Brands that incorporate eco-friendly practices and values into their ad campaigns will resonate with environmentally conscious consumers.

As we journey into this dynamic landscape, it's essential for businesses to stay informed about these trends and adapt their strategies accordingly. Embracing these developments will not only keep you ahead of the competition but also ensure that your digital advertising efforts remain effective and relevant in a rapidly changing environment. The future is full of possibilities, and the digital advertising realm is set to be more exciting and innovative than ever before.

The future of digital advertising is brimming with possibilities. By staying informed and adapting to these trends, you can position your business for success in this dynamic and ever-evolving landscape. Get ready to embrace the digital advertising opportunities of tomorrow.

Chapter 10: Conclusion

- **The Power of Digital Advertising in Business Growth**

In this journey through the world of digital advertising, you've uncovered the immense power it holds in propelling your business to new heights. The digital landscape has transformed the way we connect with our audience, and understanding the significance of this medium is key to achieving success.

Digital advertising provides unparalleled opportunities for businesses of all sizes. Whether you're a small startup or an established enterprise, it empowers you to reach a global audience, engage with potential customers, and drive growth in ways that were once unimaginable. By embracing the principles of digital advertising, you're harnessing the tools to expand your brand's reach and influence.

- **Final Thoughts and Actionable Takeaways**

As you conclude your journey through this eBook, it's essential to reflect on the insights gained and identify actionable takeaways. Here are some key points to remember:

  - Clarity of Purpose: Start with a clear understanding of your goals and objectives. Define what you want to achieve through your digital advertising efforts.
  - Audience-Centric Approach: Always put your audience at the forefront of your strategy. Tailor your campaigns to address their needs, preferences, and pain points.
  - Creativity Matters: The effectiveness of your ad campaigns relies on engaging creatives and compelling ad copy. Invest time and resources in crafting eye-catching, persuasive content.
  - Data-Driven Decision-Making: Continuously monitor and analyze your ad campaign data. Use the insights to make informed decisions and optimize your strategies for better results.
  - Stay Adaptable: The digital landscape evolves rapidly. Keep an eye on emerging technologies and trends and be willing to adapt and innovate as necessary.
  - Compliance and Ethics: Respect user privacy and adhere to data regulations and best practices in advertising. Building trust with your audience is paramount.
  - Testing and Iteration: Don't be afraid to experiment and test different approaches. A/B testing can help you fine-tune your campaigns and discover what works best.
  - Measurable Outcomes: Set clear key performance indicators (KPIs) to gauge the success of your campaigns. Use these metrics to assess your progress.
  - Budgeting Wisely: Digital advertising offers flexibility in budgeting. Allocate your resources thoughtfully, focusing on the platforms and strategies that yield the best results.
  - Continuous Learning: The digital advertising landscape is ever evolving. Stay curious and invest in ongoing learning to remain competitive.

- **Encouragement to Get Started**

It's not the size of your budget or the scale of your business that matters most in the world of digital advertising. What truly counts is your willingness to take the first step. The journey to success starts with the decision to get started.

Don't be daunted by the complexities of the digital advertising world. Instead, see it as an exciting opportunity to expand your business and connect with your target audience in meaningful ways. With the knowledge and insights gained from this eBook, you are well-equipped to embark on your digital advertising adventure.

Remember, every click, every impression, and every conversion bring you closer to your business objectives. It's time to leverage the power of digital advertising and unlock the potential for growth. So, go ahead, launch your first campaign, and watch your business flourish in the digital age. Your journey starts now!

Appendix: Resources and Tools

In the fast-paced world of digital advertising, staying updated and equipped with the right resources and tools is essential for success. Here, we've compiled a list of useful resources, blogs, websites, and recommended tools to support your digital advertising journey:

- **Useful Resources, Blogs, and Websites**

  - Google Ads Help Center (Website: https://support.google.com/google-ads)
    A comprehensive resource for all things related to Google Ads, including tutorials, best practices, and troubleshooting guides.

  - Facebook Business Help Center (Website: https://www.facebook.com/business/help)
    Get the most out of Facebook advertising with their help center, offering insights, tips, and FAQs.

  - Neil Patel's Blog (Website: https://neilpatel.com/blog)
    Renowned digital marketer Neil Patel shares invaluable insights and strategies on his blog.

  - Moz Blog (Website: https://moz.com/blog)
    Explore in-depth SEO and digital marketing resources from Moz, a leading authority in the field.

  - HubSpot Blog (Website: https://blog.hubspot.com)
    HubSpot's blog offers a wealth of information on inbound marketing, sales, and customer service.

  - Search Engine Land (Website: https://searchengineland.com)
    Stay updated with the latest news, trends, and insights in the world of search marketing.

  - Content Marketing Institute (Website: https://contentmarketinginstitute.com)
    Learn the art of content marketing from experts in the field.

- **Recommended Tools for Digital Advertising**

  - Google Ads (Website: https://ads.google.com)
    Google's advertising platform allows you to create, manage, and optimize your ad campaigns across various platforms, including Google Search and YouTube.

  - Facebook Ads Manager (Website: https://www.facebook.com/business/tools/ads-manager)
    This is your gateway to creating and tracking ads on Facebook and Instagram, giving you powerful tools to reach your target audience.

  - SEMrush (Website: https://www.semrush.com)
    SEMrush is an all-in-one marketing toolkit that provides competitive research, keyword analysis, and site audit features to enhance your SEO and content strategy.

- o Hootsuite (Website: https://hootsuite.com)
  Hootsuite is a social media management platform that simplifies scheduling, monitoring, and reporting on your social media campaigns.

- o Google Analytics (Website: https://analytics.google.com)
  Gain crucial insights into your website's performance, audience behavior, and campaign effectiveness with Google Analytics.

- o Mailchimp (Website: https://mailchimp.com)
  An email marketing and marketing automation platform to help you design, send, and analyze your email campaigns.

- o Ahrefs (Website: https://ahrefs.com)
  A powerful tool for SEO and competitor analysis, offering features like keyword research, backlink analysis, and site audit.

These resources and tools will be your allies in the dynamic world of digital advertising, helping you make informed decisions, optimize your strategies, and stay ahead of the curve. Make the most of them to drive the success of your digital advertising campaigns.

Glossary

- **Key Terms and Phrases Defined**

  Digital Advertising: Promoting products or services using digital channels like the internet, mobile apps, and social media.

  Impressions: The number of times an ad is displayed, regardless of whether it's clicked.

  Clicks: The number of times users click on an ad, leading to the advertiser's website.

  CTR (Click-Through Rate): The ratio of clicks to impressions, expressed as a percentage.

  CPC (Cost Per Click): The cost an advertiser pays when a user clicks on their ad.

  CPM (Cost Per Mille): The cost per 1,000 impressions of an ad.

  CPA (Cost Per Acquisition): The cost incurred when a user takes a specific action, such as making a purchase or signing up.

  Search Engine Marketing (SEM): Advertising that promotes a website by increasing its visibility on search engine results pages.

  Social Media Advertising: Ads placed on social media platforms to reach a specific target audience.

  Display Advertising: Graphic or visual ads displayed on websites, apps, or social media.

  Video Advertising: Promotional content in video format, commonly found on platforms like YouTube.

  Email Marketing: Sending targeted emails to a list of recipients to promote products or services.

  Affiliate Marketing: A performance-based advertising model where businesses reward affiliates for driving traffic or sales.

  Content Marketing: Creating and sharing valuable, relevant content to attract and engage a target audience.

  Demographics: Characteristics such as age, gender, income, and location used to categorize an audience.

  Psychographics: Analyzing the psychological attributes, values, and lifestyle choices of a target audience.

  Behavioral Targeting: Tailoring ads based on a user's online behavior, including browsing history and past interactions.

  Retargeting (Remarketing): Displaying ads to users who have previously visited a website but didn't complete an action.

Ad Personalization: Customizing ad content to suit the preferences and interests of individual users.

Landing Page Optimization: Enhancing a web page to improve user experience and conversion rates.

A/B Testing: Comparing two versions of an ad or webpage to determine which performs better.

Key Performance Indicators (KPIs): Specific metrics used to measure the success of an ad campaign.

Google Analytics: A web analytics service by Google to track website traffic and user behavior.

Ad Blockers: Software that prevents the display of digital ads, impacting ad reach.

Emerging Technologies: Innovations such as AI (Artificial Intelligence), AR (Augmented Reality), and VR (Virtual Reality).

Privacy Concerns: Issues related to the collection and use of user data in digital advertising.

Voice Search: Technology that allows users to search the web using voice commands.

Ephemeral Content: Temporary content that disappears after a set period, popular on platforms like Snapchat and Instagram Stories.

Sustainability in Advertising: The practice of incorporating eco-friendly and socially responsible elements in ad campaigns.

This glossary provides a solid foundation for understanding the essential terms and concepts in the world of digital advertising, ensuring you can navigate the landscape effectively.